San Antonio, City for a King

An Account of the Colonial History of San Antonio and Texas

Rudy Felix Casanova

Order this book online at www.trafford.com
or email orders@trafford.com

Most Trafford titles are also available at major online book retailers.

Printed in the United States of America.

ISBN: 978-1-4907-1560-5 (sc)
ISBN: 978-1-4907-1559-9 (e)

Trafford rev. 02/14/2014

 www.trafford.com

North America & international
toll-free: 1 888 232 4444 (USA & Canada)
fax: 812 355 4082

CONTENTS

DEDICATION

At 74, I have discerned a compelling need to manifest my appreciation for all those wonderful people before me who shared their genes—their blood, their sweat and their tears—from vein to vein, from heart to heart. And I realize that I am but a link in that vital process.

With a heart full of pride and admiration, I offer this book in veneration to my 56 Canarian ancestors who did so much to establish the beautiful community which I and my children call home: San Antonio. I also wish to acknowledge all my Isleño descendant cousins who likewise carry in their hearts those same feelings of pride and gratitude, wherever they may find themselves.

Henceforth, I dedicate this book to my five children, Deborah Anna, Richard Charles, Belinda Delfina, Melissa Marie and Marlo Yvette; and to my nine grandchildren, Melinda, Christina, Nicholas, Matthew, Jacquelyne, Jacob,

Erica, Gayle and Richard, all of whom will also continue the legacy.

Finally, I wish to honor my sisters, Olivia, Yvonne and Norma, my parents, Rudy and Hortensia and my grandparents, Mariano and Virginia Casanova, José and Gonzala Ortega, as well as all my ancestors going back to José Antonio Peres Casanova, the teenage lad from Tenerife who helped found San Fernando, La Villa Del Rey.

PREFACE

*I*nvariably, when I have shared with others some of the data that you will find in this piece, I have been encouraged to put it into print, because the information is so captivating and relevant, yet so shockingly unknown.

Historically, so many newcomers and visitors to the city have openly wondered: "Why does this city's downtown have a European feel?", "Why did the Alamo experience happen?", and "How is it that there was an American Texas in the country of Mexico, *before* the battle?"

Generally, many others who happen to hear about the Canary Islanders in San Antonio are confused as to who they were, what they did, and why what they did is not taught as history.

Sadly, most San Antonians today—even descendants of the Canary Islands Founding Families—are themselves also unaware of the city's colonial history. And in that history lie the answers to these questions.

I wrote this synoptic look at the colonial history of San Antonio because I love my beautiful city and am enamored of the history of her founders, for I am an eighth-generation descendant of at least ten of the sixteen pioneer families, and I wish to bequeath its contents to *my* descendants.

Also, I put my knowledge into prose because I felt obligated to tell the story of those Isleños (Islanders)—the 56 heroic men, women and children from Spain who risked everything to establish our lovely city for their sovereign almost half a century before the United States was born. Most cities came into being because of a river site, a crossroads or rail stop. San Antonio was created because a king wanted it to be.

It is not my intention to make a Mayflower experience of the Canary Islands pilgrims' trek to found San Antonio, but it is inevitable to question if the United States would have looked as it does today without the San Fernando experience. After all, what was ceded by Mexico at San Jacinto was that which had been San Antonio de Bejar's territorial responsibility.

Moreover, there is an inherent question when one considers the importance of this history: If San Fernando (San Antonio) had not been created, would there have been a Texas? To wit, if the town had not existed as Spanish Mexico's northernmost municipality, there would probably not have been a plan to invite Americans to settle in these lands, since it would have been quite impossible to supervise them. Without the presence of the Spanish settlers' descendants (Tejanos) or the American-Texans (Texians) in the area, there would not have been a rebellion, and in subsequence, a basis for the decisive battle at the Alamo. No San Antonio . . . no rebellion . . . no Texas.

So, allow me to highlight for you a largely unrecognized piece of Americana that, while essential to understanding the extraordinary Texan spirit, is at once one masterful stroke in the majestic tapestry of the American Southwest.

Finally, I don't pretend to have written a historical account of colonial San Antonio, for I am not a historian. I am an educator, but not a history teacher. In addition, my writing experiences have been largely in the area of journalism—in high school and college, 13 years as public information officer with the Army, and for several professional entities. Consequently, I simply amassed data and knowledge from official documents and accounts, from published books, from local Canary Islands descendants' folklore, and from naturally drawn inferences; and I have put them into print as a literary chronicle of our local history. I kept the treatment short, so that people could read it in one sitting; but I also attempted to cover as much about the story as was necessary to educate the reader in this most significant subject. Hopefully, it will provoke your interest.

PROLOGUE

There is a century of San Antonio legacy that predates the legendary Battle of the Alamo of 1836. It is an extraordinary history that shaped the fiber of the city and in turn, provided the crucible for the eventual political entity known as Texas. This genetic period has been a subject of interest, treated by historians and genealogists for decades; and yet, it is largely overlooked by popular commentators and writers of history textbooks when considering the history of Texas.

Perhaps this is due to three social factors present during the decades following the government turnover after San Jacinto. Firstly, neither the Canary Islands founders nor their early descendants had a legacy-forming mind set, so it is that they left no known memoirs for later generations. Also, the occupants of the former Spanish-Mexican town of San Fernando in 1836 found themselves overwhelmed by the unexpected task of having to adjust to, and assimilate into, the new nation called Texas. Moreover, the early

Texans were, for their part, busy building a new republic and creating a fresh history of their own.

Yet another contributing factor could be that many of the immigrants who came from Mexico at the onset of the 20th century were educated, professional people who possessed a different background than the *Isleños* and the other Spanish citizens who had migrated to the town. They altered the Hispanic society they found in San Antonio by introducing into the community their own Spanish traditions heavily mixed with a rich Aztecan culture. The result was a de-emphasis of a remarkable colonial history that engendered the Alamo City.

The bottom line is that the Canarian Experience, as well as those 105 formative years of Spanish-Mexican history that followed it, beg to be recognized and to be given their proper place in our state and national histories . . . and placed in our textbooks alongside the current Texas history treatment.

Texans may someday embrace the history found in this book and claim it for what it truly is, the real genesis of their Lone Star State. Whereas this rich legacy flows from the early Spanish colonists, it is now the inheritance of all San Antonians and all Texans since, after all, the one entity was fused into the other.

THE GENESIS

THE INITIAL SETTLEMENTS

eginning early in the 1700's, French-born King Felipe V of Spain was advised to create a civil government in the northeastern frontier of its *Nueva España,* which was then known as *Las Nuevas Filipinas.* This vast area stretched from present-day Texas west and north way beyond today's Colorado. The principal purpose was to restrain French encroachment from across the Sabine River.

For several years, the matter was discussed and deferred by the Crown and his advisors, since such a project would require heavy funding, and because finding families to volunteer for the expedition would prove difficult.

Before it became part of Nueva España, this area was called *Yanaguana* by the nomadic Payaya Indians, who used it as a seasonal encampment site because of its sources of water and mild climate.

In 1691, Franciscan missionary Damian Massanet, accompanying Governor Domingo Terán de Los Ríos on an expedition, came across the small but beautiful river, loved the spot, said Mass on it, and named the stream San Antonio, because it was June 13, the feast day of the saint. De Los Rios also called the place *San Antonio de Padua*.

On May 5, 1718, Spanish Governor Don Martín de Alarcón established *El Presidio de Béjar* (a military fort) by the river at the headwaters of the other spring in the area, *El Arroyo San Pedro*. Several families from the Spanish provinces south of the Rio Grande migrated to the site as well. Thus, they created the first European settlement there, which was to be known as *San Antonio de Béjar*. These were subsequently moved to the area just west of the river bend a few miles south.

Also in 1718, *La Misión de San Antonio de Valero* (which we know today as the Alamo) was also established on the east side of the river bend.

Yet, it was a colonization expedition finally funded and decreed by Felipe V in the late 1720's that led to the political founding of *La Villa de San Fernando* on March 9, 1731, named after the king's third and only remaining son. This single act elevated the village to the level of a town in the eyes of the Crown and its subjects throughout Nueva España.

In an era where many of Europe's royals
were interrelated, Phillip found himself heir
to both the French and the Spanish thrones;

when he opted for one, he renounced the other. Yet, his roots remained in France. It is therefore quite significant that he chose to establish San Fernando to keep the French out of Nueva España.

The missions were created as a joint venture between the Catholic Church and religious orders, primarily the Franciscans, the Jesuits and the Dominicans. They were fostered by the Spanish Government and often founded by virtue of an expedition sponsored by a prominent Spaniard. Their *mission* was to gather local Indians into a communal society within a walled compound with three major objectives: To protect the non-combative tribal populations from the warring tribes; to teach them known European skills for subsistence—farming, construction, milling, weaving, sewing, cooking, etc.—as well as martial defense; and to provide them spiritual education. Obviously, foremost was the teaching of the Castilian language. In 1726 San José de Arguayo was also established. In 1731 three other missions, La Imaculada Concepción, San Francisco de la Espada and San Juan Capistrano, were transferred from Nacogdoches and the areas of the Caddo Indians we now call east Texas to San

Antonio for reasons of security and logistics. All these were built along the San Antonio for a stretch of several miles south of the village, and where they still stand.

THE ODYSSEY AND THE ARRIVAL

Originally, the plan was to have 200 families populate the frontier outpost. Then it was cut back to 50. Citizens of peninsular Galicia and the Canary Islands, both seafaring regions of Spain, were considered prime pools for drawing settler prospects.

Nevertheless, only the initial group of ten families who were recruited in Lanzarote and a family from Gran Canaria were ever sent.

On March 27, 1730, the volunteer families, 54 citizens, from the Canary Islands answered the call to leave their homeland, traverse the Atlantic and populate a new, rustic land.

The volunteers were justifiably lured by two things: An attempt to evade an economic recession that had befallen the Islands, and a desire to experience an adventure about which they had always heard from Canarian mariners to the fabulous New World. Even though some of them had had sailing experiences, none of them had crossed the Atlantic. Moreover, most of the males in this group and none of the women and children had ever been aboard a seafaring ship.

They sailed from Santa Cruz, Tenerife on the galleon *España*, which was large in total size, but rather small to hold its crew, other travelers and all those passengers.

The weeks on board were expectantly difficult, particularly for the small children. For the most part, the sojourners behaved bravely, enduring almost constant seasickness, overcrowding, lack of hygiene, and the fear of the overwhelming nature of the high seas.

There were only a couple of incidents that allegedly occurred during the voyage. One involved a man who became so stricken with seasickness and so upset with regret over his decision to take his family abroad that he attempted to jump overboard. He had to be restrained within the hold of the ship. The other situation had to do with the oldest colonist, who had assumed the leadership of the group, but whom the captain and crew found overbearing and who often appeared to be menacing when interacting with the other group members. He also spent time constrained in the hold. On the positive side, the close quarters made for closer relationships, especially among the young travelers.

Ordinarily, a galleon was multi-level and as much as 100 feet long. The captain would travel in the main cabin above the deck. The officers and passengers—some on business, some for pleasure—would occupy cramped cabin quarters in the center area, and the crew was housed in the bow (the front section). Whatever provisions were on board would be in the galley or kitchen area. Often the ship would be transporting cargo as well. Altogether, as many as 200 people could be on the ship, making for extremely crowded conditions. What's more, the inside area could be damp, dark, smelly and attractive to rats and insects.

The colonists finally arrived safely at Havana on May 10, where they obtained fresh water and supplies.

While in Cuba, they encountered two adventuresome young brothers from Gomera who had gone to the Island a year earlier in search of a lucrative life. Some group members knew them and facilitated their inclusion into the expedition group. The men were formally granted official permission by the viceroy representative in Havana to join.

On July 9, the group embarked on a ten-day voyage across the Caribbean to Vera Cruz. For almost 2 months they were housed in that coastal city by local Spaniards by mandate of the Crown. They also acquired the necessary foodstuff, medicines, livestock, tools and supplies for their subsistence in the new land.

Regrettably, once in New Spain two adult members and a child died, presumably from repercussions from the naval journey and exposure to new deceases.

These months on the Campeche Coast were also understandably difficult for the pilgrims. They lived in unfamiliar, crammed quarters in a foreign land, exposed to unfamiliar illnesses. Several colonists were infected with smallpox and isolated. Privacy was always a scarcity, insecurity a constant fellow. And they shared a convivial existence with people who were fellow traveler compatriots at the moment, but really strangers before the trip. A third adult died during that period.

Moreover, the man who had had his second thoughts about the expedition from the beginning, disappeared when the colonists reached Vera Cruz, and he apparently took his family with him. That brought the count to only ten families in the group, the minimum number decreed by the Law of the Indies for such an expedition.

There was the ever-present fear that perhaps they had erred in their decision, and that their final destination could loom as a dire existence. And then, there were the longings for the homeland, the anguish of missing the loved ones they had left behind; assuredly, they would never see them again or hear the dearness of their voices.

Yet, they were pragmatic Canary Islanders buoyed always by their stoic faith and their unyielding hope. On the bright side, a child was born to another couple.

Also, the group gained two new members there—two brothers from Tenerife who, the previous year, had gone to Jalapa, a village near the coastal city, to work on an uncle's horse breeding ranch. When the government representative took some colonists with him to negotiate with the boys' uncle over buying horses and burros for the pilgrims, the two sets of brothers met again. Friendships were rekindled and soon the boys from Laguna, Tenerife were administratively allowed to join the group by the King's representative at Campeche.

Meanwhile, the decision was made by the Crown to have the group continue its journey over land through what we know today as Mexico rather than by ship to what today is the Texas coast, to avoid the possibility of ambush by feral coastal Indians.

The viceroy appointed Francisco Duval as official guide to convoy—with several army soldiers as a military escort—the families on their caravan. In September, the company departed from that town, with a first stop in Quautitlan to prepare for their long journey to San Antonio de Béjar . . . about 500 miles northward.

While there two other young men, one from Tenerife and the other from Palma, met the group and also asked for official inscription into the colonization expedition. They too were granted admission. These youngsters had travelled from the Islands with the four aforementioned bachelors a year earlier on a merchant galleon named "Dos Amigos". The six new members, who had known each other in the Islands, had become fast friends on their voyage to Havana. They now would become important to the group, as they could provide physical continence for them.

Moreover, almost immediately these latest bachelor enlistees would increase the number of families by two when they married two daughters of a senior pilgrim couple. Actually, the family, which was from Lanzarote, knew the boys well, as they had nursed these small-ship sailors back to health after they had been seriously injured in a shipwreck back in the *Canarias*.

Almost at the same time, yet another marriage was created by two youngsters from two other pioneer families.

Thus, began the arduous and courageous pilgrimage to the Presidio at San Antonio de Béjar. They rode on burros, on carts or on horseback, or they walked. They had weathered through almost impassable rain forests, now they trekked across treacherous mountain areas and over threateningly arid cactus lands and thick brush. The journey was painfully slow, not only because of the terrain, but also because they had to weather very cold winter spells. Of course, they suffered many illness and fatigue episodes that also elongated some of the stays.

Despite these conditions, they thrived. Two new marriages along the way increased the count to 15 families. The four remaining single men—the brothers who joined the group in Havana and the ones who enlisted at Vera Cruz—would make up a sixteenth family unit.

The wayfarers rested in over 30 small villages and in towns like San Luis Potosí, Saltillo and Monclova. Their stays, both room and board, were funded by the government. These respites were necessary to refresh both their bodies and their mental stamina. With the aegis support of Spain, their stock allocations were constantly replenished as well.

During the entire trip, Duval and the viceroy's government officials faithfully bolstered the colonists in their mission. Throughout the journey they were also accompanied by different priests who celebrated Masses and the sacraments for the families.

Meanwhile, the Canary Islanders's leader (now appointed legitimately) proved to be an assertive advocate in negotiating for the welfare of his group.

In late February, they crossed the Rio Grande—no small challenge—at Presidio San Juan Bautista. Then, they proceeded on their last stretch toward Béjar.

On the eighth of March they camped for the cold night at the Medina River, several kilometers south of their final destination. It was there that they encountered their ominous initiation into their new world, a frightful Indian raid by a small marauding band presumably looking for horses.

Luckily, the group suffered no loss of lives. However, Duval's men had to heighten their guard duties, in shifts, that night. And the *peregrinos* (pilgrims) had to make an intense effort to merely fall asleep.

How must their fears and doubts have resurged as they went to bed that heavy night!

Despite the horrifying incident the night before, the resilient pilgrims arose at predawn the following morning and broke camp for the last time. Duval had predicted that this would be their last leg and they were cautiously excited. The mere act of finally arriving at their new home after an entire year on the journey and seven rigorous months on the trail would be a wonderful thing.

Their anticipation assuredly turned to exuberance at about eleven o'clock on March 9, 1731, when they reached the presidio and the settlement of *Béjar* —perhaps on a typically beautiful, cool early spring day, sunny and with wild flowers of all hues spilling across the green, tree-filled, rolling countryside.

How swiftly their fears would have abated!

COLONIAL SAN FERNANDO

THE TOWNSHIP SETTLEMENT

When one considers the actual birth of the modern City of San Antonio the year of record is 1718, when it was established by those early settlers as San Antonio de Béjar. It was called Béjar because of the Spanish nobleman, El Duque de Béjar, who sponsored the governmental undertaking, and San Antonio because of the mission, San Antonio de Valero (Valero being the Spanish King's viceroy in Mexico City at the time: el Marqués de Valero).

The "j" in Spanish can be substituted by an "x", hence it can be Méjico or México, Bejar or Bexar; but in English, the "x" is constant in use, always Mexico and Bexar.

The Canary Islanders who arrived at Béjar in 1731 came to found a *civic* government which by decree of the Crown was named San Fernando, and thereby lent the settlement the political status of a town.

The King bestowed upon them—and on their descendants—the title of *hidalgo*, an honor that in Spanish society elevated a person in civil status making them worthy of being addressed as *Don* or *Doña*.

The colonists were quite young. The mean age of the heads of family was only 29 years. There were thirty single youths under twenty-one; the youngest was barely three months old. In Quautinlán they had been listed and basically described as being of European Caucasian stock. Some of the group were brunettes, some red-haired, some blonds. They were of fair or olive complexion, medium to tall in height, and had eyes of brown, black, green, grey or blue.

In Bejar, they were received by Captain Juan Pérez de Almazán, the commander of the presidio, and by the small group of Spanish families, known as *Bejareños,* who had set root there next to the post. They were also met by some soldiers and civilians who staffed the presidio, and their families, as well as by missionaries and Indians who lived in the mission.

Once settled in, their first official act was to lay out the town plat on the ground as decreed by the Law of the Indies, under the direction of the presidio. Of course, the leadership of the captain was essential, as the Canarian settlers were not trained in these activities.

Nonetheless, they

in the form of a squa

was assigned for th

build on the west si

sun would shine th

Around the rest o

buildings that w

and financial pr

and public safety functions.

As prescribed by the royal government,
were granted both homestead lots (*solares)* and farming
lots (they called them *labores)*. In a gesture of fairness, the
16 heads of household (fifteen actual families, and the
sixteenth formed from a composite of four bachelors). The
latter was made up of the two sets of brothers who had
joined the group in Havana and in Vera Cruz, not yet of
majority age, and not related to any of the other families.
They drew lots in a public event for their individual
homesteads. The residential land grants were established on
the north, east and south sides of the plaza between the San
Pedro and the San Antonio. The presidio was on the west
side, behind the church lot. East beyond the river bend was
the mission.

How did the mission come to be
called the Alamo? Popular lore among
the Descendants has it thus: In Spanish, a
poplar/cottonwood tree is called an *álamo*. In
the decades following the settlement, a small

either grew naturally just east
in front of the mission or was
on both sides of the road leading
the town to the mission, in European
shion. Soon the area was referred to as los
álamos (the cottonwoods). By the end of the
18th century, the mission was simply called
"*el álamo*" rather than Valero.

The family farming lots were then allocated. They
covered the peripheral areas surrounding the plaza and
the presidio and lay between the creek and the river, from
today's San Pedro Park in the north to Mission Concepción
in the south. In ensuing years, they would be granted
ranching areas that followed the river south for miles. All
this time, they demarcated for and laid down the original
streets of the city.

Somewhat hampered by the fact that, except for
two individuals, they could neither read nor write, these
otherwise intelligent and hardy survivors proceeded to
accomplish their tasks.

In the Islands, most of the *Isleños* had been fishermen,
small farmers, goat herders and craftsmen. Once here the
pilgrims focused their skills on building homesteads; and
immediately, they cleared the land and carved out their
labores (farming fields), in order to take advantage of the
spring to plant for the autumn and for the following year.

The Spanish Government furnished the group a mill.
The king appropriated each of the 16 families a small

subsidy, a yoke of oxen and the implements for tilling. Also, each family was issued the necessary clothes, medicines, foodstuff, seeds, farming and subsistence tools, and livestock to sustain themselves for the first year and beyond.

As the months passed, they began work on an ambitious construction of new *acequias*—trenches carefully engineered to carry water from the river or the creek, irrigate their *labores*, and then return it to the opposite stream. Sometimes, aqueducts were necessary. The mission Indians, who had been taught by the Franciscans how to accomplish these tasks, were then able to lead the Isleños and the other Spaniards in that effort.

> Aqueducts are bridge-like structures erected on a foundation of multiple arches and with built-in troughs on top that were used to transport water over depressions on the ground. Originally taken to Spain by the Romans, these were then brought to America by the Spanish. At least one aqueduct from that era survives in the city.

The two brothers who had joined the party in Jalapa, Vera Cruz had apparently acquired an affinity for the crafts of equine husbandry and ranching. Providentially, this aptitude proved to be of significant advantage to the settlers in the early years and to Texans in the future.

As all emigrants, the Canarian pioneers must have missed their homes and families in Europe; but reading between the lines of legal documentation accounts, generally they appear to have been very happy in their new environment, and they began to form their new lives by creating new families and new ways of bartering by raising essential crops and livestock . . . particularly chickens, hogs, goats, cattle and horses.

Those very crops that these early settlers farmed then—corn, tomatoes, peppers, watermelons, squash and cotton among others—and the ranching practices they instituted almost 300 years ago are still part of present-day San Antonio and its surroundings.

With the protection of the presidio personnel, they were able to secure their crops and livestock fairly safe from periodic raids by Comanche from the north and Apache from the west. Also to take into account, all those young immigrants assuredly afforded the group encouraging stamina, despite their inexperience.

Initially, the settlers were housed on the premises of the presidio. In time, they began the task of constructing their first family residences. For the walls, they used available clays and mud, small timber and rock. The roofs were generally thatched. These were known as *jacales*. In later decades the jacales were replaced by sturdier wood and adobe structures.

Mail, foodstuff, medicine, dry goods and other supplies required long, tardy wagon trips from Saltillo, Querétaro, Guanajuato and other distant cities south of the big river.

In the former years, the Islanders prepared their favored dishes from their homeland, but as the decades passed and certain ingredients became difficult to procure, they readily adopted the indigenous foods from the interior (today's Mexico), modified them to their taste, and formed their own cuisine.

> **One of the dishes they developed with old country and new world *chiles* and meat ingredients was a spicy stew they called *chiles con carne*, which a century later became known simply as "chili".**

THE CABILDO (TOWN COUNCIL)

*T*he *cabildo* is a civic council still in use in the Canary Islands by which the different islands sent representatives to a central executive body. On the first day of August of 1731, Captain Almazán, gathered the married male heads of family to initiate the *Cabildo de La Villa de San Fernando.* (The Spanish government officially sanctioned this action on October 24.)

Juan Leal Goraz was chosen as the *alcalde* (mayor) of the Villa, and five others were appointed *regidores or consejales* (aldermen or councilmen), namely: Juan Curbelo, Antonio Santos, Salvador Rodriguez, Manuel de Niz, and Juan Leal, Jr. Even so, during the initial years most of the leadership was carried out by Leal Goraz, supported by Almazán and assisted by José Padrón.

Actually, Goraz, who personally helped recruit several of the families back in the Islands, had served as the universally accepted head of the group throughout the entire expedition. And Padrón had been his loyal right hand.

As prescribed by the edict, five men were then selected to fill administrative offices: Juan Leal Goraz as a *juez* (judge), and Salvador Rodriguez as his *diputado* (deputy judge), Vicente Travieso as *alguacil* (constable) to keep the peace and enforce the laws, Antonio Rodriguez as *mayordomo* (tax collector/treasurer) to collect and manage the revenues of the city, and Francisco Arocha as *secretario del consejo* (city clerk) to keep minutes of council meetings and to serve as a notary public. Travieso and Arocha were the only two who could read and write fluently. They were the two young men from Lanzarote who had joined the group in Quautitlan.

Many of the petitions and some of the findings had to be heard or ratified by the governor, but they were all administered in the presence of the local judge and recorded by the secretary.

The cabildo governed over all the inhabitants of the villa: The Canary Islanders, the presidio civilians, the Béjar residents, the occupants of the missions and any other Spaniard that happened by. All of the men were appointed by Captain Almazán for life. They all served diligently for decades to settle civil disputes and land allocations, as well as criminal cases occasioned by a growing population and altercations arising from Indian episodes. Together, they nurtured La Villa de San Fernando into a town worthy of seating a Spanish Governor in 1767.

The [city] council form of government has survived for almost three centuries as the form of civil government in San Antonio; and it has served as a model for many municipalities in Texas and beyond. Every August, descendants of the *Canarios* celebrate the establishment of the Cabildo with a Mass at San Fernando.

FOUNDING OF SAN FERNANDO PARISH AND CHURCH

*W*hen the Isleños came, they brought with them their Catholicism; and with their religion, they brought their patron saint, Mary, in the image of *La Virgen de la Candelaria*, Our Lady of the Candlemas. Even though a provision was made coincident with the founding to establish a parish for their religious needs, during the former years the Families were served spiritually by missionaries from de Valero, and subsequently, from San José. They would hear Mass there or in the presidio. They were also administered by visiting priests from the interior.

In 1738, after a string of fund-raisers and donations mostly from the Families—and with materials and the labor of members of the Families as well as from borrowed artisans—the parishioners finally broke ground for their parish church. Yet, it took 11 years to complete the structure, because of persistent funding problems.

The church was finally blessed on November 6, 1749. By then, the Canarians had become devotees to Our Lady of Guadalupe as well, so the new church was dedicated to the Virgin Mary under her two titles important to them.

They named it San Fernando, like the town, in a show of allegiance to King Felipe and reverence to his son. It was consecrated after the Catholic monarch, Saint Ferdinand III, who did much to free Andalusian Spain of the Moorish occupation in the 1200s, united Castilla and León, founded several orders (including the Franciscans) in southern Spain, and was canonized in 1671. A portion of the original structure still forms the west end of the present church, although the dome had to be replaced in 1873. In the floor of this domed chapel still honoring Mary in her two titles is implanted a metal plaque indicating the copular, geographic center of the city. Sadly, in 1828 a fire destroyed much of the structure, and with it, many of the church records. In the 1870s, the present church was erected in the gothic style.

In August, 1874 San Fernando became the cathedral for the new bishopric of the Roman Church in San Antonio; and in August, 1926, the see (diocese) was elevated into an archdiocese. Today, San Fernando is still an active parish church in the downtown area, the oldest continuous parish in the United States.

Some of the original settlers were buried around San Fernando. Subsequently, the parish constructed what is today known as Milam Plaza as its cemetery. Early Isleños were originally buried there but later exhumed and buried elsewhere.

Immediately upon the initiation of the cabildo, the priest of San Fernando began a practice still observed today, and that is that each incoming city council is blessed by the rector. This practice, in recent years has grown to be an ecumenical event shared by religious clergy of all faiths and denominations of Saint Anthony's city.

Current descendants of the Founding Families celebrate the feast of the *Candelaria* every February and the *Llegada* (arrival) every March with a Mass in the cathedral.

The cathedral, with its surviving *Plaza de Las Islas* (Main Plaza) in front of it, has been the social and cultural heart of the village of Béjar, of the town of San Fernando, and of the city of San Antonio, for more than two and one half centuries.

THE LEGACY

EVOLUTION OF SAN FERNANDO

*F*rom its inception, San Fernando, aka San Antonio, has always attracted to itself peoples from other communities. In the early years, when compatriot Spaniards, Creoles (persons born in the New World of Spaniard parents) and Indians migrated to the township from ranchos and settlements south of the city, the town leaders quickly learned to govern over its transplants as well as its native citizens.

Through the decades, the Canarian colonists constructed the *Casas Reales* and other civic infrastructure and facilities necessary to conduct the business of running the town. They even built a jail to house perpetrators of infractions and felonies. Unfortunately, through the ensuing decades, some of these structures had to be rebuilt.

Many of the streets and roads that were laid out then are still in existence and in use today, though many have been renamed in English.

There were many significant events and accomplishments during the ensuing years, such as the seating of the regional governor in San Fernando to preside over a vast northeastern area of *Nueva España*.

Unfortunately, they continued to suffer raids from the Apache and from the Comanche. In the latter part of the 18th century, however, a transplanted New Mexican, Francisco Chaves, and a French immigrant, Pierre Vial, effected a historical peace treaty with the Comanche Nation in the name of the Governor, Domingo Cabello. This one act dramatically eased relations between the many tribes from the north.

> Chaves was kidnapped from Albuquerque by the Comanche at the age of eight and taken to the area that today forms parts of North Texas and South Oklahoma. There he learned to speak or understand several Indian dialects, a talent that served him well in San Fernando to win asylum and the Spanish governor's sponsorship in his late teens, as well as to accomplish the aforementioned treaty. He married Juana Padrón, a daughter of one of the Founding Families, and quickly became a respected soldier and citizen. In

the 1800's, his granddaughter, Virginia Chaves, became the wife and ex-wife of the notorious "Judge" Roy Bean in San Antonio. She later married Manuel Charles. They had a daughter, Virginia, the author's paternal great-grandmother.

Local folklore maintains that when a most significant treaty was accomplished, the Indians buried a live horse with a hatchet on its back in the plaza as part of their ritual. Hence, the phrase, "bury the hatchet".

Canary Islands descendants' folklore portrays the settlers as true to their homeland's love for enjoying life and having good times. They held fiestas to celebrate their Canarian holidays, particularly the Feast of the Candelaria on February 2. In addition, they celebrated Christmas *posadas* (Mary and Joseph searching for room in Bethlehem), as well as Holy Week passion ceremonies and Easter festivals. Then there were the church wedding, baptism and birthday *fandangos* and *fiestas* (apparently, they loved fiestas). And in later years, charreadas and *rodeos became popular.*

In time, the raising of cattle for subsistence turned into the occupation of ranching for some. When ranching became prominent in the San Fernando area, *rancherías or haciendas* (ranching settlements) came into existence in the areas south, east and southwest of the town. Before long, as friendly rivalries between the *rancheros* developed, the *charros or vaqueros* —ranch hands who worked with the *vacas (cows),* hence cowboys—competed in *charreadas* or *rodeos*. These impromptu skirmishes soon became public events at fiestas.

A few years ago, a leading Japanese car manufacturer gave San Antonio's economy a significant boost by establishing an assembly plant in its southern edge. The location proved to be the land originally granted by Spain to the family of one of the pilgrim brothers from Tenerife (and Jalapa) for a ranch. The site, sold by the then current heirs, sits close to the Medina River, near its confluence with the San Antonio River.

During the first generations in San Fernando, the sixteen families basically coalesced when celebrating these events. They shared in their moments of joy and in their times of grief. Their offspring married each other's children, baptized each other's babies and mourned each other's dead as personal family.

Eventually, they mixed with the other brother Spaniards—both peninsular and locally born—who had settled in the San Fernando area, in its surrounding areas, and in the southern territory all the way to the Rio

Grande. The village of La Bahía, later named Goliad, was a prime sister city going south on the San Antonio. Many of those settlers had also been awarded land grants from the Spanish government through the years. In the 1770's some families were displaced from Nacogdoches to Bexar. Once the missions were secularized, the Indians also became natural marriage options. Throughout the latter half of the 19th century, the Spanish-Mexicans from south of the Rio Grande joined the mix.

As the population of the township grew, new situations befell the citizens. From time to time, San Fernandoans requested new land grants from the government. Some argued over taxation matters, others experienced land disputes against squatters, and occasional draughts caused farming distress which led to significant water distribution disagreements. Misdemeanors and felonies began to keep the judge and the constable busy; so, eventually they were awarded suitable monetary compensation.

Although the weather did not seem to be a problem for the Bejareños, they did have to cope with the annual *canícula*, a two-or-three-week period of high heat during mid-summers. Also, one known coastal hurricane apparently did heavy damage to the new villa.

During the years following the Texas Revolution, San Antonio experienced considerable growth both in size and in prominence, as immigrant groups from European countries such as Germany, Belgium, Poland, Ireland, France and Italy settled in the region. These newcomers, who largely shared the Catholic faith with the original settlers, made a rather smooth transition into the society. Yet, they maintained their individual communities and customs, until the 20th century. Meanwhile, they were instrumental in establishing the city's commercial structure and banking business, and in converting the practices of farming and ranching into actual industries. In the latter 19th century, Jewish settlers also helped to establish a mercantile practice in the community.

> It is said that when Hispanic women served in Jewish households they learned to make their unleavened (pita-like) bread. And when they imitated the recipe at home with added ingredients of fat and leavening, they created the popular flour tortilla, a staple in San Antonio cuisine until today.
>
> As mentioned before, some of the items of the cuisine developed by early San Antonians were adaptations and modifications of Mexican and Spanish dishes, like corn tortillas, tacos, enchiladas, menudo, tamales and salsas. Twentieth century San Antonio *Tejanos* introduced other recipes which have delighted the American palate, such as *fritos* (corn chips), nachos, carne guisada, picadillo, green enchiladas, fajitas, puffy tacos and, of course, the notoriously popular flour tortilla tacos. All this has come

to be known as Tex-Mex food rather than San Antonio food, but they really are innate of San Antonio's unique flavor.

San Antonio music is also said to have started as a composite blending of Canarian, Spanish and Mexican strains and instruments. In the mid-1800's, the German settlers shared their polka beat and the accordion with the Hispanics, who then created a Latin polka, which in the early nineteen hundreds became *conjunto* (ensemble) music, the forerunner of today's Tejano music.

SAN FERNANDO AND THE AMERICAN WAR FOR INDEPENDENCE

*D*uring the American Revolutionary War of the latter 1770's a most significant mission came to the early Isleños and the other early Tejanos who had settled in ranches and towns from Bejar to La Bahía.

In addition to making important loans to the colonists, Spain came to the aid of the American colonists by assigning to the Spanish Governor of Louisiana, Bernardo de Galvez, the critical role of denying to the British access to the Mississippi.

To help feed his large military force and in turn aid the Continental Army, the Spanish government petitioned the ranching families of Tejas who, of course, were Spanish subjects, to provide Galvez with thousands of head of cattle during several years. They complied. But, how would they get the beef to Louisiana? They put on their sombreros, their *chaparreras* (chaps) and *espuelas* (spurs) and rode them all the way there . . . the first cattle drives in what is today the United States . . . about a century before the cowboy era.

Through this venture, San Fernando—therefore San Antonio—became a recognized contributor to the American Revolution, a distinction enjoyed by only a very few other American cities west of the original thirteen colonies. It also affords the descendants of those *rancheros* a possible membership in the Sons and in the Daughters of the American Revolution.

SAN FERNANDO'S CIVIL WARS

*T*he early generations of the Canary Islands settlers had to endure two civil wars in the early 19th century.

First, there was the war of independence from Spain in the 1810's, which pitted brother against brother and neighbor against neighbor, because one would be loyal to the crown and the other to the rebellion. For the Canarians, there was a particular reason for discord: Spain did not allow them to trade with their neighbors in the Louisiana territory, many of whom were Canarian Hispanics. This issue was important to the isolated Isleños because, while the mainland trading centers were so far south, their Louisiana cousins were much closer and had direct contact with Europe.

It took months for word of the organized movement in Central Mexico to reach San Fernando. Nevertheless, once aware, the *Bejareños* (common appellative for all San Fernandoans) got fully involved. Several significant skirmishes were fought around the city between the

Crown's soldiers and the rebels, among them the Alazán Creek, Rosillo Creek and Medina River battles.

> An interesting aside: It is reputed that when Miguel Hidalgo, the priest who called Mexico to battle with his famous *grito* on September 16, 1810, was being pursued by the Spanish loyalist army after that event, he set out for San Fernando for safety. Unfortunately, he was captured en route and subsequently executed.
>
> Interestingly, a young Mexican lieutenant made a name for himself at Medina: Antonio López de Santa Anna.

Meanwhile, Spain was weakened by her distraction with French encroachment in the mainland and by other rebellions in Latin America. The end result was that she proved unable to maintain her grip on the Aztec nation; and so, when the smoke settled in 1821, Mexico was born, and San Fernando became Mexican. This, of course, means that when San Antonio celebrates Mexico's Independence Day, *el Diez y Seis de Septiembre*, it is celebrating its own solemn history.

Some of the descendant soldiers and loyalists found themselves unable to remain in San Fernando after the change of government and they moved to family ranchos in the open country or to other communities where other immigrants had settled, like Goliad, valiant Goliad. Some migrated to Louisiana, where there was another Canary Islands settlement.

The second rebellion was the war of independence from Mexico in the mid-1830s. For the Mexicans in general, the major point of discontent was Santa Anna's push toward his autocratic rule of the nation. Specifically, the struggle with the central government on the part of the citizens of San Fernando (and the region of Coahuila) began in the mid-20s. It was based on over-taxation, under-representation, lack of protection from Indian raids (the presidio was no more) and trade issues. The insurrection, as we now know, grew into an amalgamated effort with the newly settled Texian imports.

> Toward the end of its hold on the region, Spain had granted permission to some American citizens to settle in the Tejas region. Then, when he became president of the new republic, Santa Anna continued to permit some of them to settle in and develop land parcels specifically deeded to them in the Tejas territory. The invitees would generally become Mexican citizens, abandon slavery practices and adopt the State religion. The project worked well for the settlers. Soon many others in the United States and beyond began to answer the call and emigrate to Tejas on their own. So it is that these newcomers considered themselves

full citizens (Texians) and beholden to
struggle alongside the Tejanos. Conversely,
the Mexican president took umbrage at that.

By 1835, the discord had developed into a martial
campaign and the Texians had begun to share leadership
roles with the Tejanos in an anti-Santa Anna campaign.
The President, therefore, faced an insurrection by his own
citizens and a challenge by immigrant settlers.

Several incidents occurred between the impassioned
Tejanos/Texians and the valiant Mexican soldiers in towns
like Goliad and Gonzales and in San Fernando. The most
critical were the Battle of Concepción (the mission) and
the Siege of Bejar, which led to the surrender of General
Martin de Cos.

Cos was at once, the Capital's representative in Béjar to
supplant the rebellion and the president's brother-in-law.
This abdication is believed to have provoked the
Commander-in-Chief's deployment into San Fernando
and the resultant pivotal Battle of the Alamo, which
happened the following March, when brave men on both
sides carried out their horrendous missions—one group
had to combat a much larger army, the other had to scale
the walls of a fortress.

Many wonder if the native
Spanish-Mexicans of San Fernando were
even participants in the revolution, since,
as popular history tells the story, they seem

to have been absent at the Alamo. The fact is that they *were* there and they *did* die in the Alamo, yet not in large numbers because they were regrouping to secure other areas.

On the Tejano side, there were six Hispanics among the hundreds of volunteers who rose to legendary heights during the revolution. Juan Sequín, a San Fernando mayor, led a cavalry unit alongside the Texians at San Jacinto. José Navarro, native Bejareño, resigned his post as the Tejas and Coahuila Deputy to the Mexican Congress to join the cause and eventually sign the Texas Declaration of Independence. Lorenzo de Zavala, who resigned his post as Mexico's Diplomat at Paris to become a rebel, became the first Vice President of the new Lone Star Republic. José Francisco Ruiz was an officer in the first revolution against the Mother Country, a respected Cabildo councilman in San Fernando and a signer of the Texas Declaration. Gregorio Esparza and Toribio Losoya were heroes of the Siege of Bejar in December and combat mortal casualties at the Alamo in March. (Unlike the others who had died at the mission, Santa Anna allowed Gregorio a proper burial, in response to the plea of his brother Francisco, whom the general had known in San Fernando during the first revolution.)

NOTE: Jim Bowie, a Kentucky-born transplant businessman from Louisiana who went to San Fernando in 1828, became a Mexican citizen, a Catholic and the son-in-law of the governor of Tejas seated at San Fernando. Had he survived the battle, perhaps the city would have had in him a Texan champion with political stature and clout after the transition of governments.

One Texian of the era who figured prominently was Bejar resident Samuel Maverick, who later served as mayor of San Antonio. He became a successful rancher who refused to brand his cattle, and when stray, unmarked beef were found, they were assumed to be from his stock, so they were branded a "maverick", a term that has come to mean *independent.*

The Texians had formed a sizeable militia throughout Tejas that, when coalesced with the Tejano forces, formed a formidable foe for *el Presidente.* The war ended with the birth of yet another new nation, the Republic of Texas, when Mexican President Antonio de Santa Anna surrendered at San Jacinto and later signed the Treaties of Velasco.

THE CANARIANS IN
THE NEW STATE

When the Creole descendants of the Founding Families and their latter New World-born Spanish settlers resorted to rebellion against Mexico, they envisioned a continuation of life as independent citizens. After the Texan victory, they found themselves as citizens in a new jurisdiction administered in a foreign tongue. (The city was also renamed San Antonio.)

Consequently, for the second time in one generation, some descendant families found themselves wanting to leave their beloved township. Again, a few moved to places in Louisiana where other Creoles lived. Many simply occupied their *ranchos* and *solares* around the missions. Others resettled in new communities farther south along the river or in other parts of the new republic. (During the latter half of the 19th century, the author's own grandfather and great grandfather, both, were born and raised in their ranches, in an area now known as Elmendorf, Texas.)

Nevertheless, some of the former Tejanos, now Texans, enjoyed high and venerable offices in the new order.

And San Fernandoans participated in the pivotal Battle of Salado Creek in 1842, primarily under Captain Salvador Flores.

> From August 1, 1731 until September 18, 1837, the Mayors of San Fernando had all been Spanish or Spanish Mexican. On September 19, 1837, the first Texian mayor of San Antonio, John W. Smith, took office. Smith married an *Isleña* descendant, María Jesusita Curbelo and begot five children, forming one of the first bi-ethnic families in the Alamo City; their descendants are numerous today. (Smith is regarded as a Texian hero. He was the man who was sent from the mission, before the attack, to alert the other Texians, and thereby, spared death by Santa Anna's troops.)
>
> From January 9, 1841 to April 18, 1842, Juan N. Seguín, who was, at different times, celebrated as both a Tejano and a Texian hero, served as mayor. Thereafter, all the mayors were non-Hispanic, until Henry G. Cisneros assumed the office on April 4, 1981, after a landslide election.

Ultimately, most descendant families remained in the central town to help mold a new San Antonio society, which has since flourished into the cultural blend of peoples of different genealogical roots that permeates the city today.

One more chili note: Sometime during the former half of the 19th century, some Hispanic women took their very affordable, spicy concoction out of their houses and unto the plazas of the city to sell to late-night and all-night revelers, as well as to early risers. After the Civil War, when down-and-out **cowboys** drove the cattle of South Texas to the railheads of the Midwest, they often relied on these ladies' food stands for their meals. These women, who have become widely known as the "Chili Queens of San Antonio", were actually pioneering in offering Mexican food in public places. (The cowboys, meanwhile, were paid when they got to their destinations; and once with money, they were able to afford steaks . . . which is probably how those places became popular for their cuts of beef.) The "queens" continued their practice well into the 1930s, when they fell victims to public progress . . . the city's new health office's regulations.

Taking into account their subsistent role in the American Revolution, it can be stated that the Canarian descendants of the Founding Families have been participants in every war in which the United States has been involved.

Returning from the Second World War, hundreds of San Antonio Hispanics came back from military duty convinced that Latino kids needed to rise in social stature by learning to speak English sans accent and by educating themselves in the higher levels. This started a renaissance that has led to such prominence for the San Antonio Hispanics that they are represented in every trade, craft, profession and political office present in the Alamo City, including the hierarchy of the Church.

Through the decades of the 19th century, the Isleños' descendants married other European immigrants. In many cases, many of them—especially the Polish and the Belgian—made an effort to adapt to the local Hispanic culture by learning Spanish and its cuisine. During the turbulent years of the 1910 Mexican revolution many more Latinos escaped to San Antonio and provided more marriage opportunities for the founders' descendants.

In the latter half of the 20th century, they found non-Hispanic Americans from other parts of the country to marry, particularly the many who were stationed in one of the five military bases in the city.

Today's descendants of the sixteen Canary Islands founding families are ushering in their 13th or14th generations and they number in the legions. Surprisingly, quite a few of them have maintained their Spanish lines pretty much intact.

Nevertheless, because of the marriages that occurred during the 5th, 6th, and 7th generations with immigrants from Mexico, many Canary Islands descendants today have become accustomed to being called "Mexican-American", since after all, they have been classified into that minority category for demographic purposes. They are often referred to as "Latinos" also. And they are included in the "raza" expression, an epithet which is based solely on the connotative meaning of the word in Spanish—the people, the brotherhood—not the denotative, race.

Yet their apparent preference—if they must be signaled out from mainstream Americans—is the current term "Hispanic", for that reflects their basic ethnicity. Although most of them still live in San Antonio and the surrounding Texas areas, many live in cities throughout the United States. Furthermore, large numbers of the current descendants do not have Spanish surnames, nor do they speak Spanish. What's more, they bear the appearance of, and live as, non-Hispanic (Anglo) Whites. Whatever the case, all these descendants carry the pride of their Canarian ancestry in their hearts, and they instill that pride in their descendants . . . even if they may not be completely aware of their beautiful legacy.

EPILOGUE

$\mathcal{N}$otwithstanding the world-renowned emblematic relationship between San Antonio and Texas and their Alamo, the fact is that there is an unique and impressive colonial history of San Antonio, the city whose history precedes the creation of the Republic of Texas by over one hundred years; the city that gave the illustrious Lone Star State its genetic birth.

The city came to life three centuries ago, when the Spanish established a fort called *San Antonio de Béjar* there. A few civilian families accompanied the military and formalized the *Yanaguana* area with a European settlement. Later, the Mother Country sent several families from Europe to the site to create a civil township in accordance with the Crown's specifications. The king's city was named *San Fernando* but, out of force of habit, many in *Nueva España* continued to refer to the settlement as *San Antonio de Béjar,* or simply, *Béjar.* On December 14, 1837 the City was officially renamed *San Antonio.*

San Antone was the tag of choice of the post-Civil War newcomers who came to the town looking for work in the cattle industry, manned the cattle drives northward, became the English equivalent of *vaqueros*—cowboys, and rode into the nostalgic American "West" era. The nickname was used for more than a century, but the frontier town has grown to over a million citizens and is counted as the seventh largest city in the United States. Oddly, it is often described as a large small town. Perhaps this is because its pace, like its river, is meanderingly tranquil. It could be due to the fact that its quality of life is unabashedly provincial. Some suspect that it's because its commercial attitude, while aggressive, tends to be unpretentious.

Nevertheless, a fruitful outcome of its natural charm is that it has become a preferred tourist destination, because, as visitors say, "people are genuine there, and friendly".

A barometer of San Antonio's lifestyle is her enduring love for a city-wide celebration. Her eleven-day April "Fiesta", for example, by which it has been celebrating herself for 120 years, is a first-rank, full-blown *fandango* replete with over one hundred major events that bring together hundreds of thousands of volunteer workers and millions of joyful party goers and fun-loving spectators. Seriously committed faux royals reign over fairs, shows, bazaars, cultural festivities, competitive fetes, carnivals, *charreadas* and multi-hour-long parades—on streets and on the river, in the daytime or at night. All the time and everywhere there is the wonderful food of San Antonio in open fare, like the Chili Queens of yore. The entire fiesta is a familial affair driven by good-natured fun and wholesome camaraderie, none of the bizarre. "Fiesta City" is a well-deserved moniker for her.

There are several other major, city-wide celebrations held almost every month, like the world renowned 19-day rodeo in February that celebrates the city's Western legacy and attracts the best cowboy performers and Country and Tejano entertainers, as well as almost two million visitors.

Cinco de Mayo is always reason for another giant fiesta. It honors Mexico's liberation from French occupation in the 1860's and is the largest of numerous ethnic festivals that celebrate the many diverse cultures of the cosmopolitan city.

The Texas Folklife Festival in June is a Texas-sponsored composite celebration of the confluence of cultures that has formed the unique society of the state. It draws thousands of artists and participants from throughout the state who participate to represent their personal ethnic experiences via food, song and dance. Hundreds of thousands of visitors—both locals and tourists—attend to savor the cultural diversity of the Lone Star State.

Each Labor Day, a leading national magazine recognizes the role of San Antonio in the evolution of Spanish influence in the States; and so it puts on, there, an annual celebration with world-wide exposure that is designed to showcase the vibrant Hispanic culture in this country. A score of top-notch international Latino artists are brought to the city to perform. The weekend fandango draws visitors from throughout the world.

> In 1955, the very first television station in the United States to broadcast totally in Spanish, KCOR, was established in San Antonio. This station soon grew into the ground-breaking Spanish network, SIN. This is the forerunner of Univision, which was initially headquartered in San Antonio.

Again, when San Antonio celebrates *El Diez y Seiz de Septiembre*, Mexico's Independence Day, it does so because the city continues to maintain a very close relationship with Mexico. But San Antonio also observes its own unique legacy each 16th of September—its own actual combative contribution in the struggle for freedom from Spain in the early 19th century. So the city-wide *pachanga* (blow out), replete with *desfiles* (parades), *ferias* (fairs) and *fiestas* (parties) is a meaningful event.

The city lies in the south-central heart of today's Texas. It enjoys a symbiotic relationship with its river, which is recognized internationally for the mystical segment called "The Riverwalk". Some say the stream defines the town and so they call it *River City*.

Others say *The Alamo City* is a more defining epithet for San Antonio because of the pivotal battle of the Texas Revolution. Nonetheless, while the Alamo is, by and large, venerated as the vanguard of Texas heritage, the city of San

Antonio appears to have become somewhat like the oyster that renders its precious gem, and then is overshadowed by its own yield.

Even so, it is not altogether disregarded, for it has been affectionately called "every Texan's second city". However, all that said, San Antonio is neither overtly appreciated nor officially recognized as Texas' *natal city*.

Today, the city occupies three quarters (over 400 square miles) of Bexar, the county named after her ancient name. As much as it has grown, *S.A.* (its modern tag) retains its particular personality and it is often considered one of the unique cities in the country. When the many newcomers settle in, they generally become assimilated into the San Antonio persona rather than change the city's character. Even the San Antonio Spurs—the good guys who do their best and take life as it comes, with no heart for flagrant boasting when they excel or for hot-headedness when they fail—manifest her way of being within the National Basketball Association!

In short, charismatic S. A. appears to be quite happy in its own skin.

Something to consider is that though it was Spanish for a century and heavily influenced by Mexican culture after that, other ethnic groups have done much to mold the city's character. In the 1850's, the German Americans, for instance, basically established its commercial industry, while the Belgian and the Polish newcomers joined with their Spanish brothers later in developing the San Antonio area farming practices into an industry. And, there have been many others: The Italians, the Irish, the Lebanese, the French and the Chinese. Over the decades, these peoples shared their architectural, linguistic and culinary nuggets to create an admirable blending of cultures and a truly unique urban entity.

Also to acknowledge, the hundreds of thousands who have relocated to this metropolis throughout the decades from all parts of the country and from foreign lands pursuing employment or a better way of living. Many "adoptees" have claimed they visited the city on holiday or for convention, loved the place, went back to where they came from to pack their belongings, and then returned to stay.

African Americans have historically formed a rather small percentage of the city's population, but they have served as an essential element in its social melding. Their influence in today's San Antonio is such that over 100,000 citizens participate in the Martin Luther King march each January.

In addition, the thousands of military personnel who have passed through the city's five installations since even before the Civil War—in peace and in wartime, for training or for development—and felt genuinely embraced by the community have, in turn, left their mark on it, and they have labeled it as *Military City, USA*. The city, in turn, includes the military in every major civic function and celebration.

Why Military City? We shall remember that the 1718 initial settlement of San Antonio happened concurrently with the establishment of the Spanish presidio, which endured until 1821. As early as the 1840s, the city hosted military personnel before, during and after the Mexican War, the Civil War and the Indian wars. In 1885, the Apache chief and hero Geronimo, was held prisoner at the installation which, in 1890, was formally inaugurated as Fort Sam Houston. During the World War I years, Fort Sam Houston and Brooks Field in San Antonio played important roles in training the initial flyers who eventually manned the Army Air Corps, which in turn, became the Air Force. These three Air Force bases in Military City—Kelly, Randolph and Lackland—were established in 1916, 1930 and 1942, respectively and have been celebrated for their excellent contributions to military flying. Randolph trains many of our pilots while Lackland trains our airman recruits. Fort Sam is home to military medicine personnel of all branches.

City of Missions is a sacrosanct name for San Antonio, as it embodies the spirit of the iconic missions that first pierced its skyline almost 300 years ago and are still standing majestically in their Spanish splendor.

The mythical Texas cowboy, which for generations marked the Texan character, had much of his roots in: "San Antone". The nostalgia of the late-1800s era of "the West" was in part initiated by the *vaquero* personage and the legendary *arreadas* (cattle drives). These young men engaged to walk South Texas' *ganado* (cattle) from S.A. to parts north; and along the way, they left their imprint on San Antonio's character, too.

Lastly, in the 1950s local *Chicanos* (a vernacular derivative of Mexicanos, when pronounced Me<u>chi</u>canos) came up with their own endearment title*: San Anto*. Since the 90's, a local organization has borrowed that term to identify its barrio sub-culture endeavors. Another such appellation is *San Quilmas*, popular with local lowriders.

So it is that San Antonio, which had both humble and regal Spanish births and numerous names, has acquired from multiple ethnic imports. Yet, the salient reality is that it always shows her Hispanic soul within her American countenance.

The author relates the following as an epiphany which first prompted him to define his birth city to others:

A few years ago, I was disembarking from a ferry at Sausalito and looking back at the magnificent city scape of San Francisco, when two men and a woman, doing the same thing, began to make remarks. One man said, "This has to be the most beautiful city in the States." The other man said, "I think it's New

Orleans. The woman then said, "I love San Antonio." Immediately, the men chimed, "Yes, of course. San Antonio is gorgeous." "You're right." I was almost dumbstruck, but so proud to learn that others thought so highly of my lovely plebeian city. I came back and saw my town with different eyes.

In San Antonio Hispanism is innate, genuine, natural and vibrant because of her physical and cultural proximity to Mexico. Visitors from Latin American and European countries enjoy a welcoming American environment there, while they feel a kinship in the local ambience. Likewise, American tourists from other states go there and enjoy the charming Latin flair while in their very own country. The reason . . . the city's rich colonial past, for it is *La Villa del Rey, The King's City.*

THE FOUNDING FAMILIES

1. *Juan Leal Goraz (54) Lanzarote (widower of Luisa [Lucía] (45), who died while in México)*

2. *Juan (50) Lanzarote y Gracia (46) Curbelo*

3. *Juan (son of Juan and Lucía)(30) Lanzarote and María Gracia (30) Leal.*

4. *Antonio(50) and Isabel (34) (Lanzarote) de los Santos*

5. *José (22) Lanzarote and María Francisca (20) Padrón*

6. *Manuel (50) Gran Canaria and Sebastiana (44) de Niz*

7. *Vicente(25) Tenerife and María Ana (daughter of Juan and Gracia Curbelo) (18) Travieso (married in Mexico, en route)*

8. *Salvador (42 Tenerife)and María (42) Rodríguez*

9. *Francisco (27) La Palma and Juana (daughter of Juan and Gracia Curbelo) (14) Arocha (married in Mexico, en route)*

10. *Antonio (18) Canarias and Josefa (daughter of Manuel and Sebastiana de Niz) Rodríguez (married in Mexico, en route)*

11. *José (22) (son of Juan and Lucía) Lanzarote and Ana (15) (daughter of Antonio and Isabel de los Santos) Leal (married in Mexico, en route)*

12. *Juan (19) Lanzarote (son of Lucas and Mariana) and Catarina Delgado (15) (married in Mexico, en route)*

13. *José (15), Marcos and Ana Cabrera Lanzarote (children of Juan and María, who both died during the trek from Vera Cruz)*

14. *María Robaina Bethencourt Rodríguez Granado, (widow of Juan, who died in México, en route)*

15. *María Meleano Delgado Lanzarote (30) widow of Lucas [Luis], who died in Mexico, en route)*

16. *Ignacio (24) and Martín Lorenzo (20) de Arma, brothers, Gomera, (who joined at Cuba) and brothers Felipe and José Antonio Pérez Casanova**, Tenerife, *(who joined at Vera Cruz)*

*The list of members of the expedition compiled in Quautitlán lists the second set of brothers as Pérez; however, there are numerous documents cited in the Bexar archives in which José Antonio identified himself as *Pérez-Casanova*.

THE CANARY ISLANDS

The Canary Islands form one of 17 autonomous regions of today's Spain. As an autonomous region, they enjoy the right to make some governmental decisions independently, particularly when it comes to foreign trade and cultural exchanges.

An archipelago of seven large islands—Lanzarote, Fuerteventura, Gran Canaria, Tenerife, Gomera, La Palma, and El Hierro—and six small ones, they lie in the eastern Atlantic.

Around the first century before Christ, the Romans discovered the archipelago and found a large quantity of large native dogs, *canis* in Latin, inhabiting the islands . . . from whence came the name *canarias*. That is why their flag bears two dogs guarding the blue (the Atlantic) shield (with the seven islands) and (Spanish) crown.

Many myths have been associated with the islands, including the one that suspects that they are the remaining peaks of the lost continent of Atlantis. Also native to the isles is a breed of birds, most of which are yellow. They were given the name "canary" because of the islands, not the other way around, as many think.

The *human* natives of the islands was a group of people described by visiting Europeans as strong, tall, blond, light-colored eyes and very handsome . . . the Guanches, found primarily in Tenerife.

According to legend, one day a wooden statue in the form of a woman floated unto their beach. At first, they attempted to dispose of it, but when the idol *miraculously* prevented its demise, they took it ashore, built a grotto for it, and began to venerate it. When the Spaniards arrived, they identified the statue as the image of the Virgin Mary of the Candlemas, popular throughout Europe as a depiction of the presentation of the Christ (the Light of the World) at the temple and the purification of the Madonna. Some theorize that the statue may have belonged to a shipwrecked Portuguese ship. This solitary relic served as a pivotal facilitator in the conversion of the Guanches to Catholicism and Christianity. The Founding Families brought their patroness with them. Although Italians, French and Portuguese—even the Turks—explored the territory during the Middle Ages, they have been Spanish since the middle of the 15th century.

The islands are situated approximately 70 miles due east of Morocco . . . curiously, on the same latitude as San Antonio. Also, that distance is roughly equivalent to the distance between San Antonio and Austin. In addition, the distance (as the crow flies) from the Islands to the Spanish mainland is about the same as that from Amarillo in the northern point of the Texas panhandle to Brownsville in the southern tip.

The total population of the Canaries today, estimated to be just over two million, compares with that of the San Antonio metropolitan area's population.

The climate of the Canaries varies from island to island because of the differences in topography. Some are mountainous, particularly Gomera, where the people developed the *silbado*, a whistling language, as a method of communicating from crest to crest that was much faster than land travel and is still practiced. Others have piney woods. Still others are tropical and balmy,. But they all have beautiful beaches . . . to the point that they have become favorite vacation spots, as well as retirement destinations, for northern Europeans.

The Canary Islands have two capitals, Santa Cruz, Tenerife and Las Palmas, Gran Canaria; and the President, the Canaries' highest government official, must alternate his or her official seat between the two cities every four years. Politically, ethnically and in religious affiliation, Canaria aligns fully with Spain and the European community.

In the past, Canarians were known to emigrate to other destinations, primarily to Latin America and other parts of Europe Lately, other peoples have been immigrating *to* the Islands . . . mostly from the northern countries of Europe and of northwestern Africa.

Because the Canary Islands government cherishes its ties to San Antonio, it has maintained contact with the city for several years. Personalities in the cultural, educational, civic and entertainment arenas visit San Antonio and the founding families' descendants in an exchange of *afecto*.

RESOURCE FOUNTAINS

Buck, Samuel M. "Yanaguana's Successors", 250th Anniversary Commemorative Edition, Copyrighted by Robert M. Benavides, San Antonio, 1980.

Castañeda, Carlos Eduardo, "Our Catholic Heritage in Texas", 7 Vols. Austin, Von Boeckmann-Jones, 1936.

Chabot, Frederick C. "San Fernando: The Villa Capital of the Province of Texas", San Antonio Series, Number IV, Naylor, San Antonio, 1930, Printed 2006 by Paso de la Conquista, San Antonio.

Chabot, Frederick C. "With the Makers of San Antonio" Privately Published San Antonio, 1937.

The author acknowledges much admiration, indebtedness and gratitude toward:

John Ogden Leal (posthumously), Canary Islands Descendant of Juan Leal Goraz, and Canarian cousin of the author who, as Bexar County archivist, spent years translating San Antonio colonial documents from Spanish to English, thereby facilitating the efforts of scores of students and writers, and who shared much in amazing conversations with the author.

To learn more about:

. . . Canarian descendants, visit:

A) CIDA-SA. org

B) San Antonio Founding Heritage
   502 Adams
   San Antonio, TX 78210

. . . Relationship between San Antonio and Canary Islands, visit:

Friends of the Canary Islands

. . . Tejano History, visit:

Texas Tejano Championing Tejano Heritage and Legacy

Or e-mail at www.texastejano.com

. . . Galvez and the American Revolution, visit:

Granaderos y Damas de Galvez

. . . Genealogy of San Antonio, Bexar, Texas, visit:

Los Bejarenos Genealogical and Historical Association

"Living very happily in San Antonio's West Side barrio
in the 1940's", says the author, "I grew up thinking
I was one hundred per cent Mexican American. And
even though my paternal grandfather always made it a
point to stress that we were Canarians, I had no notion
of my Spanish genealogy . . . until my later years."
He joined the Canary Islands Descendants
Association in the city, and learned from hundreds
of Canarian "cousins" about their unique legacy.
He served as president for three terms, during which time he
delivered many public speeches to audiences that were, he
says, surprisingly interested and hungry for the magnificent
history of those brave founding families from Spain.

Made in the USA
Middletown, DE
23 November 2015